I0412176

TABLE OF CONTENTS

ACRONYMS

APMS   Assistant Professor of Military Science

CGSC   Command and General Staff College

COA   Course of Action

HRC   Human Resources Command

MCoE   Maneuver Center of Excellence

MMAS   Master of Military Arts and Science

OCS   Officer Candidate School

ROTC   Reserve Officer Training Corps

USMA   United States Military Academy

ILLUSTRATIONS

TABLES

CHAPTER 1

INTRODUCTION

Background

US Army maneuver battalions carefully manage the few incoming African-

American Second Lieutenants to ensure that they are spread across the organization as

well as possible. Often there is only one black maneuver field grade officer in most

brigade combat teams. This study investigates why so few African-American male cadets

choose one of the maneuver branches as his branch of service. Research reveals that the

reasons African-Americans do not choose Infantry or Armor have been known for at least

the past 15 years (Butler 1996, Burke 2002, Doward 2008). Cultural differences, career

aspirations, and ―negative perception of combat arms branches‖ deter many African

American cadets from choosing Infantry or Armor as their branch of choice (Burke 2002,

iii).

The Army as an institution has invested in diversity in both its enlisted and officer

ranks, but has been unsuccessful in solving a problem unique to such a small population

of its overall force. Thus, the issue remains that few African Americans choose Infantry

or Armor as their branch of choice. The purpose of this study is to propose and analyze a

way the Army may address the shortage of African Americans choosing maneuver

branches.

Research Question

The primary research question is derived from COL Ronald Clark‘s Master of

Military Arts and Science (MMAS) thesis ―The lack of Ethnic Diversity in the Infantry:

Why Are There So Few Black Infantry Officers in the US Army?" (Clark 2000). COL Clark suggests future research on —the role of mentors and role models in the pre-commissioning process and marketing strategies to increase the ethnic diversity of combat arms branches (Clark 2000, 73-74). Thus, the primary question this study addresses is: is mentorship an acceptable, feasible and suitable way to increase the number of African American male cadets that choose Armor or Infantry as their branch of service?

This question is approached by answering secondary questions:

1. What are the reasons that African Americans do not choose Armor and Infantry in more significant numbers?

2. Why is mentorship a suitable way to address low African American accession into the maneuver branches?

3. Are the risk associated with implementing a mentorship program mitigated enough to make it an acceptable option to maneuver leaders?

4. What affects the feasibility of implementing a maneuver mentorship program within the pre-commissioning nodes?

Thesis

The Army, Accessions Command, and the United States Military Academy are recruiting African American officers into the Army at a rate proportional to the African American percentage of the US population (Maxfield 2009). Thus, it may not be in any of these organizations' interest to apply resources (fiscal or manning) to address African American under-representation in Infantry and Armor. The onus of increasing African American participation in the maneuver branches therefore, falls to the branches themselves. They, operating in a wartime environment, have been unable to implement effective measures to correct the phenomena.

In order to increase Armor and Infantry accessions of African American officers, the Maneuver Center of Excellence (MCoE), along with the Human Resources Command (HRC) should consider attacking the problem with a maneuver branch implemented formal mentorship program. This mentorship course of action (COA) includes assigning successful African American maneuver branch officers to Reserve Officer Training Corps (ROTC) and United States Military Academy (USMA) positions in direct contact with cadets. These role models will participate in a formal mentoring program designed to increase the number of African Americans choosing the maneuver branches as their military occupational specialty.

The factors that keep maneuver branch accessions of African Americans relatively low are historical and cultural in origin. In the Army's recent counterinsurgency efforts, cultural and historical influences are most effectively influenced by exploiting a single narrative communicated at all levels of influence (FM 3-24 2006). The delivery strategy for the maneuver force in this case is mentoring. Mentoring may be most effective if conducted by maneuver officers conveying a consistent narrative touting the virtues of being a member of the maneuver force. The narrative used can be developed by analyzing the motivating factors that drive African American cadets' choice of branch.

Assumptions

This study assumes that the current trend of low African American officer participation in Infantry and Armor will continue unless there is some institutional fix applied to address the issue. No societal influences alone, such as the economy, support for conflicts, or citizens' view of the Army will ameliorate the problem.

Definition of Terms

For the purpose of this study, the term African American refers to African American males. The term excludes females because Department of Defense policy currently precludes females from branching Infantry or Armor.

Several terms unfamiliar to the civilian population are used throughout this document. Maneuver Branch is a division under the Maneuver, Fires and Effects career field (HRC 2010). The branches or occupational specialties designated as maneuver are Infantry, Armor, and Aviation. For the purposes of this study, maneuver or Maneuver Branch is defined as Infantry and Armor.

Aviation is excluded because that branch does not produce the same number of general officers as the other two branches. Currently none of the Army's active duty Generals came from the Aviation branch (GOMO 2010a). Nine of the twelve Generals were formerly branched Infantry or Armor (GOMO 2010b). The significance of this study lies in the ability of African American officers to attain positions in the highest echelons of the Army structure. Currently the path to the majority of those positions lies within service in the Infantry or Armor branches.

Pre-commissioning sources include the Army ROTC, the USMA and Officer Candidate School (OCS). Through ROTC and USMA, cadets receive pre-commissioning training while attending college (Cadet Command 2011). Upon receiving their bachelor's degree, the cadets are then commissioned as officers in the Army. There are also ROTC programs which allow an officer to be commissioned with an associate's degree.

4

OCS is a shorter program of instruction that admits Soldiers who already have an associate's or bachelor's degree. These candidates are trained over a number of weeks and are commissioned into the Army upon graduation. Due to the relatively short amount of time that cadre have to influence OCS candidates, this pre-commissioning source is largely omitted from this study.

ROTC is run by Cadet Command and accounts for approximately 45 percent of yearly officer accessions. USMA, which accounts for approximately 17 percent of a cohort, reports directly to the Department of the Army and not to Cadet Command. OCS, which provides the remaining 38 percent of new officers a year, falls under the command of the Infantry School at Fort Benning, Georgia (Wardinski, Lyle, and Colarusso 2010, 10). The number of new officers commissioned each year is determined by the needs of the Army, but in recent years the Army has commissioned approximately 6400 new officers in a fiscal year (Wardinski, Lyle, and Colarusso 2010).

Limitations

This study is limited by the amount of time and resources available to the author. CGSC's MMAS program operates for approximately eight months and funds for students to travel to different destinations to conduct research are limited. Therefore, in- depth interviews or surveys with current cadets, Professors of Military Science, or Tactical Officers is not possible. ROTC and Government Accountability Office data provides demographic data and the results of surveys conducted on behalf of the Department of Defense about students' military career preferences.

Previous studies on this topic are limited and largely consist of MMAS theses and Army War College Monologues. Much of the data in this study is gleaned from previous

MMAS papers, studies by Cadet Command, and various government studies on diversity in the Army. There is significant literature on mentorship that is used to help develop a feasible program.

Scope

This study assesses the suitability, acceptablility and feasibility of targeting African American male cadets for recruitment into the maneuver branches through formal mentorship programs, and examines the implications of the policy for ROTC, USMA, and the maneuver branches. This study does not address recruiting African Americans into ROTC, USMA or OCS because all sources of officer accessions are currently meeting their diversity goals. This research does not address a program to keep African Americans in the maneuver branches once they have been accessed as such. The scope of that topic requires another full study.

Included in the scope of this study is a review of the historical and cultural elements that contribute to African American non-selection of Infantry or Armor as their branch. Tenets of successful mentorship and how the maneuver branches might incorporate those tenets into a formal mentorship program addressing the historical and cultural elements are also integral to the scope of this research.

Significance of This Study

Of the 12 Generals (four stars) currently serving in the active-duty component of the Army, nine were promoted from either Infantry or Armor branches (GOMO 2010a). These are the men that lead the Army on the Department of the Army staff or Combatant Commanders for all US forces in different parts of the world. Two of these Generals (about 20 percent) are African Americans and both were Infantry officers (GOMO 2010b). In the next subordinate rank, Lieutenant General, there are 50 officers, 26 of whom were Infantry or Armor (GOMO 2010a). These are the Army's primary staff officers at the Army Staff level in the Pentagon, commanders of Army Corps, and various other major commands. Only three of the fifty are African Americans and none of those three were in the maneuver branches, which statistically makes them less likely to be Generals in the highest positions of authority in the Department of the Army (GOMO 2010b). Having so few African Americans at these ranks, in these positions, makes the Army susceptible to a perception by African American Soldiers, civilians and others that there is no place at the higher echelons of the Army for African American Officers. This is neither a perception that the Army deserves, nor one that it has worked for.

If African Americans do not choose to serve in the branches that comprise the majority of the highest ranks in the Army, then the chance of an African American attaining those ranks is lessened because of the normal attrition of officer cohorts. Therefore, to increase the probability of African Americans attaining the general officer ranks, Infantry and Armor branches must find ways to attract more African American cadets to these branches. If this is not accomplished, then the pool of outstanding young officers who choose to serve in the maneuver branches is diminished at a time when the need for such officers is high.

A lack of diversity in Armor and Infantry branches may decrease the African American community's opportunities for promotion to general officer and foster the perception that the maneuver branches are hostile to African Americans. Alternatively, attracting more African Americans into Infantry and Armor should eventually increase the number of African Americans who attain the general officer ranks and lessen the negative perception of the two branches that African Americans may hold. This effort could also make future African American cadets more comfortable with choosing a maneuver branch, because they see more ethnicity in those occupational specialties.

Chapter Summary

The lack of African American officers in Infantry and Armor branches has been a topic of study since 1996 when Lieutenant Colonel Remo Butler wrote the research paper ―Why Black Officers Fail" (Butler 1995). CGSC theses have since addressed the question repeatedly and the continuing trend of low African American accessions into Armor and Infantry led Cadet Command to conduct its own research into the phenomena (Huggins 2010). Statistics and the purported causes of this issue have remained consistent over time and are accepted by the author of this study. The scope of this study is focused on a proposed COA that addresses the issue of low African American accessions. Chapter 2 reviews the evolution of the African American cultural attitude toward service in the Army, the elements of culture, tenets of mentoring, and civil-military relations theories that are be applicable to the problem.

CHAPTER 2

LITERATURE REVIEW

Introduction

Low African American participation in the maneuver branches is a result of the greater African American community's perception of the Infantry and Armor branches and the utility of service in these specialties in civilian life. This chapter begins with a historical overview of African American participation in the Army from the post-Civil War era through Vietnam. This history is important because it traces how the attitude toward service in the Army's maneuver branches changed over time in tandem with the socioeconomic and political change that occurred over this same period within the United States. An understanding of the history and its effects provides a better understanding of the current African American culture that largely eschews service in Infantry and Armor. The next portion of the chapter then describes the current situation pertaining to this research.

Previous studies by the RAND Corporation, government agencies, Army War College and CGSC students describe the problem that the maneuver branches are suffering and recommendations for addressing that problem. The second portion of the chapter provides a synopsis of the data these studies produce. Several studies mention the cultural issues explained in the historical portion of this chapter, therefore the next section details the organizational cultural model that this study uses to frame the problem. Lastly, the definition and tenets of mentorship as defined by Army doctrine is addressed to provide a broad overview of the factors to be considered when establishing a mentorship program that attacks the cultural issues deterring African Americans from choosing Infantry or Armor as their branch of service upon commissioning.

<u>History of African Americans in the Army</u>

Just as the evolution of a group's perceptions can be traced through their shared experiences, so too is it with African American perception of and attitude about service in the United States Army. This portion of the chapter describes how and why the motivations for African American service in the Army evolved from obtaining freedom to attaining socioeconomic status. Each conflict from the Civil War to the Vietnam War is covered briefly explaining the social and political factors that affect the African American community's perception of service in the Army. Lastly, the evolution of thought about the African American's service in the Army from the point of view of the United States government is described in the same manner.

The African American Community's Motivations for Serving:
Civil War to Vietnam

African American service in the military historically seems to have been more a means to a social and economic end than an act of overt patriotism. African Americans historically have an equal amount of love of country as the rest of the population, but they also served to prove that they were worthy of equal treatment.

During the Civil War, a major impetus for African Americans to serve was freedom to enjoy the fruits of democracy. Civil War Medal of Honor winner, Sergeant Major Christian Fleetwood summed up the feeling best: ―A double purpose induced me and others to enlist, to assist in abolishing slavery and to save the country from ruin" (Wright 2002, 91). Once the war was over and all the slaves were emancipated, African

10

Americans served primarily because of the economic benefits of Army service. This remained the impetus for service from Reconstruction to the Vietnam War. The purpose of service in the Army to advance civil rights was not introduced in literature until World War I (Moskos and Butler 1996).

Reconstruction to World War I

After the Civil War and the disbanding of the state militias in which most served, African Americans were relegated to serving in one of four regiments: the 9th and 10th Cavalry and the 24th and 25th Infantry. For the most part, they served in these units only as enlisted men, chaplains or doctors. The only three black officers who managed to graduate from the United States Military Academy during this period served in these units as lieutenants, but none led troops in combat during this time (Wright 2002). Reenlistment rates and the low number of desertions demonstrate that African Americans were happy to be serving.

During the Spanish-American War, African Americans readily volunteered to serve, but there was a small schism within the African American community about service in the war. This is the first instance where the idea of complete willingness to serve in the military at the whim of the US government was challenged. Some African American anti-war activists stressed that taking part in a war against Spain only increased the chances that the United States could impose its racist system on the non-white population of Cuba. Spain had not enacted such a system (Franklin and Moss 1994, 298).

Similar sentiments remained within a small segment of the African American community up to and through the Vietnam era and may be a factor in why a segment of the contemporary African American community refuses to serve in the Army or if they

11

do serve, seek to do so in branches that are perceived to not actively participate in closing with and destroying the enemy.

World War I represents the first time that African American officers were permitted to be trained in any significant numbers and the first time that most of the Army specialties became open to them. Pushed by the recently formed National Association for the Advancement of Colored People (NAACP), the War Department determined that it would establish a ROTC training camp for African Americans at Fort Des Moines, Iowa. —On October 15, 1917, at Fort Des Moines, Iowa, 639 African Americans were commissioned-106 captains, 329 first lieutenants, and 204 second lieutenants" (Franklin and Moss 1994, 327). Franklin and Moss depict combat experiences of the African American combat units placed under the control of the French army, but they do not mention that the larger proportion of African Americans who joined the Army at the time were assigned to more menial tasks (Bosco 2003, 57).

Editorials in African American publications during World War I showed how the impetus for service in the Army during war had evolved into one containing the desire improve the overall perception and situation of African Americans in the United States (Nalty and MacGregor 1981). Service was not only seen as a way to earn a living but also as a means to gaining the equality that the community yearned for. W.E.B DuBois, one of the founders of the National Association for the Advancement of Colored People, sums up the sentiment thus:

> This is a crisis of the world. For all the long years to come men will point to the year 1918 as the great Day of Decision, the day when the world decided whether it would submit to military despotism and an endless armed peace-if peace it could be called-or whether they would put down the menace of German militarism and inaugurate the United States of the world.

We of the Colored race have no ordinary interest in the outcome. That which the German power represents today spells death to the aspirations of Negroes and all darker races for equality, freedom, and democracy. Let us not hesitate. Let us, while this war lasts, forget our special grievances and close our ranks shoulder to shoulder with our own white fellow citizens and the allied nations that are fighting for democracy. We make no ordinary sacrifice, but we make it gladly and willingly with our eyes lifted to the hills. (Dubois 1918, 77)

Despite their efforts, African Americans were disappointed at war's end. Their participation in the nation's military provided almost nothing in return in regard to African Americans' rights at home. Mark Ellis, the author of *Race, War and Surveillance: African Americans & the United States Government During World War I*, expands on African American disillusionment with the US government during WWI (Ellis 2001).

He directly addresses the African American attitude toward service in the military during this time period and presents the most comprehensive picture of African American dissension during the war. Ellis' work sums up the attitude against service in WWI with a quotation from a former editor of an African American newspaper: —fail to see how I can conscientiously volunteer to fight for a _World Democracy' while I am denied the fruits and blessings of a Democracy at home" (Ellis 2001, 45). This sentiment, when combined with the sentiment of people such as DuBois, shows the origins of the duality of the African American attitude toward military service.

African American service as enlisted men and officers in the Army, post Civil War through WWI, was motivated initially by pure patriotism, but the motivation evolved to include a means to prove that they were worthy of equal treatment in the United States. Advances such as being allowed to serve in branches other than infantry and cavalry, and gaining the right for officers to be trained in large numbers in ROTC, were offset by the injustices of Jim Crow and the reprisals meted out to African American Soldiers who dared hold their head high upon return from the theater of war. This experience helped to increase the negative attitude toward military service in the African American culture. This trend of African Americans not receiving their just dues within the American society while faithfully executing their military duties continued through the Civil Rights era. This phenomenon is important to the analysis of this study because it helps to identify the root causes of the African American narrative as it pertains to military service.

The early history of service clearly demonstrates the fact that the African community can be just as patriotic as the other segments of American society. This is in contrast to data presented in a Marine Corps slide presentation shown at Harvard that showed the African Americans were almost half as likely as whites to consider themselves as Very Patriotic (King and Volpe 2008, 22). History also subtly implies that the personal, tangible value of service in the Army, and in the maneuver branches must be demonstrated to the African American community.

World War II

The World War II era in America witnessed marked advances for African Americans in the Army. Political pressure and necessity paved the way for the initial, limited desegregation of the Army and the use of African American combat units by the US in actual combat. African American officers also made strides. WWII ushered in the first African American general officer and postwar efforts led to African American officers being assigned to positions of leadership within the regular army. This period also witnessed increased agitation against injustice and segregation in the military and in civilian life.

African American units established during WWI bore a large share of unit reductions after the war. —By 1940 ther were less than 5,000 African Americans in an army composed of 230,000 enlisted men and officers. Only four black units, the Twenty-fourth and the Twenty-fifth Infantries and the Ninth and Tenth Cavalries, were up to full strength" (Franklin and Moss 1994, 434). African American reaction to the reduction of African American forces was not as conciliatory as it had been in previous conflicts. The reduction and other slights on the home front caused the community not to support the government as wholeheartedly as it had before.

Dr. Rayford Logan, a Howard University professor and NAACP advisor, explained to congress that the African American attitudes toward military service were of three thoughts. One was that African Americans should be accepted into the military without discrimination or segregation. The second thought was that African Americans should not serve in the military at all because they were not privy to all the rights afforded the white citizens of the country. The last thought was that African Americans should serve in the military despite the institutionalized racism that existed in order maintain the freedoms that the country offered in principle and to do their part in the war effort (Logan 1941).

These —trains of thought" are the evolution of the positive sentiments of men such as W.E.B. Dubois for African American service in the nation's military and the negative opinions of men such as A. Philip Randolph, a civil rights leader and union organizer, who refused to —go alng in all-out support of the war" (Franklin and Moss 1994, 345).

Despite sentiments regarding service in the military, African Americans participated in the military effort in numbers proportional to their population in the United States. African Americans still regarded service in the military as a means to attain equal treatment, although they served in segregated units. It also still served as one of the better economic opportunities for African Americans at the time (Myrdal 1944, 421).

The Korean War

The Korean War's surprise and casualty rate finally ended the Army's segregation policy. The Eighth Army originally deployed with four African American units: the Twenty-fourth Infantry Regiment, the Seventy-seventh Engineer Combat Company, the 159th Field Artillery Battalion, and the 512th Military Police Company (Wright 2002, 209). These units were placed in the larger Eighth Army to adhere to the War Department Army Circular 124's mandate that smaller sized African American units be placed in larger white units to achieve the Army's preferred version of integration (Nalty and MacGregor 1981). As casualties mounted, the small size of the US force mandated rapid infusion of replacements which did not allow for the segregation practices of the previous world wars. Commanders accepted individual African American replacements directly into their units without segregating them from their white counterparts. In 1951, after a formal request by Gen. Matthew B. Ridgeway, Commander-in-Chief Far East, the Army Chief of Staff finally ordered the integration of the Far East Command. This led to integration in other theaters of command in subsequent years until 1954, when the last segregated unit is the Army was disbanded (Nalty and MacGregor 1981).

The full integration achieved in the Army did not decrease the amount of racism that African Americans Soldiers experienced. Integration in civil society had not taken

16

effect at all. Thus, African American political leaders and the community began to agitate more forcefully for their rights as citizens. The expectations of the community created by desegregation of the Army were not achieved in reality, thus the negative attitude toward military service established itself more prominently. In the African American community the full effect of this negative attitude would manifest itself in the unwillingness of African Americans to volunteer for service during the Vietnam conflict.

Vietnam

Struggles in the civilian sector affected the military during the Vietnam conflict and this is where change in the African American attitudes about service in the military occurred. African American officer candidates were no longer barred from selecting any branches of service, but racial strife during the Vietnam conflict discouraged many African American college students from even wanting to join ROTC (Johnson 2002).

Blacks now had vastly greater opportunities open to them, and a select few were rapidly climbing into positions of greater authority. But the perception of the majority who remained at the bottom would eventually be that those opportunities were limited in reality if not by policy. By the late 1960s, with America again at war and the military again finding itself host to a large number of new recruits, that perception would become widespread among black troops (Wright 2002, 223).

Despite the demonstrations, protest and the resurgence of Jim Crow in the late 1950s and throughout the 1960s, African American service in the Army was still proportionally high. African Americans reenlisted at twice the rate of whites (Franklin and Moss 1994). In short, although African Americans disagreed with the domestic and

17

foreign policies of the government, the military still presented one of the few opportunities for socio-economic advancement for the community at the time.

The sentiment that service in combat arms, perceived as inherently more dangerous than other fields, was not prudent since such service garnered little social reward spread to the wider African American community. The slighting of the African American community gave voice to demonstrators who had for years been discrediting selfless African American service in pursuit of rights. Selective reporting further added to the negative perception of African American service in the military.

A 2009 RAND study restates a widely held belief that African Americans bore a disproportionate amount of risk of being war casualties (Lim et al. 2009, 9). This is based on data from 1961 to 1966 (Berryman 1988, 81). However, a government study conducted in 1971 reported that 11.9 percent (29,677) of Soldiers serving in Southeast Asia were African American. The cumulative army African American portion of deaths by hostile action by 1971 was a slightly higher 13.2 percent (3,916 persons) (OSD 1971). The two percent disparity in African American combat deaths in Vietnam has fomented a perception that remains extant and may be a cause of African American aversion to military service and service in maneuver branches (Lim et al. 2009, 9).

Firsthand accounts in the book *Bloods* (Terry 1984), show that African Americans in combat units in Vietnam thought that they were doing more fighting than their white counterparts. This perception was acted upon shortly after the war's end due to African American agitation. The Army sought to reduce the number of African Americans in combat arms and increase their numbers in combat service support branches (Pentagon 1975). An article in the ―Equal Opportunity Current News," a DoD publication, outlined

18

an Army plan to increase African American officer numbers and specifically decrease the number of African Americans in combat arms to ─broaden minority opportunities in the Army across the board" (Pentagon 1975, 1). An editorial in the same publication details the importance of ─noncombat, prestigious, career-building positions" to African Americans (Williams 1975).

The African American community's desire to use the Army as a professional stepping-stone marks a further evolution in the community's reasons for service in the Army and suggests that Army policy helped to create the dearth of African American officers in the maneuver branches. Whereas African Americans joined the Army for socioeconomic advancement and civil rights until the Vietnam era, it is clear that once they achieved some semblance of civil rights, socioeconomic factors became the community's main reason for advocating service. American history demonstrates that the attainment of one's rights may necessitate the sacrifice of blood, but if one's goal is improvement in social status, then the risk of injury or death (which is perceived as more likely in maneuver branches) is not as acceptable. African American individuals perceived less utility of service in the Armor or Infantry, than in the more technical branches.

The Present

The Army has produced successful African American enlisted Soldiers and officers who serve in all of its branches. Since Vietnam, African American participation in all sources of commissioning grew and eventually reached a level commensurate with their representation in the US population. But the primary motivator for African American service in the Army has further evolved into the attainment of career enhancing skills for use in increasing their earning potential in the civilian sector. Representation in the maneuver branches is low. The reasons for African American underrepresentation, as interpreted by previous studies, are addressed in the next section.

Recent Studies on Why African Americans
Do Not Choose Maneuver

Unlike the study of African Americans in the enlisted ranks, research specifically concerning the African American demographic in the officer corps, and the disparities with which those officers serve in different branches is not expansive. Therefore this study uses the consensus of multiple Army War College, School of Advanced Military Studies, and CGSC research projects as a point of departure. This is possible because the few published reports on the subject by Cadet Command and the RAND Corporation corroborate the findings of the academic studies. The findings fall into two categories: difference in cultures and lack of proper mentorship.

Remo Butler's, ―Why Black Officer's Fail in the U.S. Army" (1996) is a foundational compilation of research on African American officers. Butler's Army War College research project concludes that the failure of African American Army officers is due to the difference in military education received by African American cadets, inadequate mentorship offered to African American officers, cultural differences hindering those cadets' success, and lastly the ‗Good Old Boy Network' (Butler 1996, 21). Other research works on the topic come to the same general conclusions and most expound on the mentorship aspect whether it be before entering college, during college or post commissioning (Doward 2008, Burke 2002, and Harney 2000).

Elements of Culture

This study examines the feasibility and suitability of developing and implementing a mentorship program that elevates the virtues of service in the maneuver branches within African American sub-culture of pre-commissioning sources. The perceptions, beliefs and thus actions of African American cadets cannot be influenced without such a program. Since the primary target of this paper is the Army community, the study uses the same model of organizational culture that is taught at CGSC. African American culture as it pertains to service in the Army is depicted within this framework to explain how African American culture impacts the problem of low African American representation in the maneuver branches.

Lesson four of the Intermediate Level Education course's leadership seminar is —Organizational Culture and Climate." The scope of this lesson provides students with —a solid understanding of the difference between organizational culture and climate, the means for assessing and influencing climate, and the overall effects of culture on an organization's climate" (L100 2010, 125). Organizational culture is taught using the model espoused by Edgar H. Schein (Schein 1992).

Schein depicts culture as having three different levels: Artifacts, Espoused Values, and Basic Underlying Assumptions. The definitions of each level and their relationship to each other are shown in figure 1.

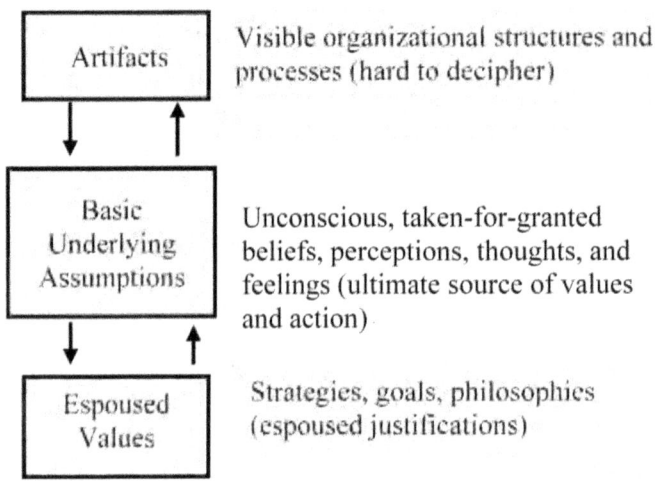

Figure 1.   Levels of Culture
Source: Edgar H Schein, —Organizational Culture and Leadership," in L100, *Developing Organizations and Leaders* (Ft. Leavenworth: US Command and General Staff College, 2010), 134.

The Artifacts are the actions or symbols displayed by a group that one can observe. —Fopurposes of cultural analysis this level also includes the visible behavior of the group and the organizational processes into which such behavior is made routine" (Schein 2010, 134). Espoused Values are the philosophies and strategies of a group that are based on basic underlying assumptions. Schein states that some values are formed by the shared experiences of the group. These values also can help to develop assumptions held by the group. —I these realms the group learns that certain such values, as initially promulgated by prophets, founders, and leaders, work in the sense of reducing uncertainty in critical areas of the group's functioning. And as they continue to work, they gradually become transformed into nondiscussable assumptions supported by articulated sets of beliefs, norms, and operational rules of behavior" (Schein 2010, 137).

Basic Underlying Assumptions are beliefs, or thoughts shared by a group that can dictate the actions of individuals in that group. These assumptions are formed over time as similar results occur in a group's shared experiences (Schein 2010). Critical to this thesis is the following:

> culture change, in the sense of changing basic assumptions is, therefore, difficult, time consuming, and highly anxiety provoking. This point is especially relevant for the leader who sets out to change the culture of the organization.

> The most central issue for leaders, therefore, is how to get at the deeper levels of a culture, how to assess the functionality of the assumptions made at each level, and how to deal with the anxiety that is unleashed when those levels are challenged. (Schein 2010, 144)

Changing basic assumptions is critical because this paper's primary question is how to get more African American cadets to choose Infantry or Armor as their branch of choice. The study addresses this question by examining the assignment of maneuver leaders to commissioning sources to be among the culture of African American cadets. These leaders' mentorship is the key to changing basic underlying assumptions about Infantry and Armor.

Mentoring

The Army's definition of mentorship is found in Field Manual 6-22, *Army Leadership* (2006); ―the voluntary developmental relationship that exists between a person of greater experience and a person of lesser experience that is characterized by mutual trust and respect" (8-14). In the Army manual, the term mentor is often accompanied by the word ―coach" and "counsel." The word mentor is the precise term for this study because it pertains to advising someone in terms of their future. Counseling is used for discussing the past while coaching is done to help a protégé during the present as depicted in the figure 2.

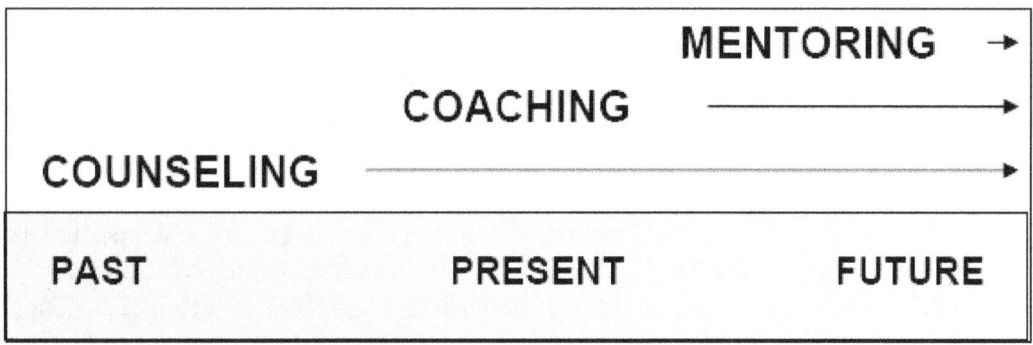

Figure 2.   Leadership Tools Compared over Time
Source: Ted Thomas, Ph.D, and Jim Thomas, *Mentoring Coaching and Counseling: Toward a Common Understanding* (Ft. Leavenworth: US Command and General Staff College, 2010), 4.

While the Army's manual states that mentors who have had similar experiences or backgrounds as the young leaders being mentored may be more effective in their mentorship, it does not count similar background as a mandatory component of the mentor-mentee relationship. Though similar background, ethnicity, or occupation is not a prerequisite, it can be helpful to establishing a positive relationship (Ensher and Murphy 2005). There are also dangers in same-ethnicity mentorship in an organization (Johnson and Ridley 2004). The more important key to the relationship between the mentor and the protégé is that they are compatible. Both parties need to find mutual comfort in the formal or informal relationship to get the most out of the experience.

Most authors describe both the mentor's and the mentee's or protégé's role in mentoring. This study focuses on the role of the mentor and how a mentor selects a protégé, and the mechanisms by which the mentor develops and influences that protégé over the course of the pre-commissioning curriculum.

Competing Theories of Civil-Military Relations

Germaine to this study is the question of the military's responsibility to the civil sector. There are competing theories on the military's role as an actor in social change. Two of the primary theories in American civil-military relations are the Liberal Theory (Huntington 1985) and the Republican Theory (Janowitz 1960). Both theories maintain that the primary role of the military is to provide for the nation's security under civilian control, but they differ in how each allows for civilian _interference' in military matters (Snider and Carlton-Carew 1995).

Samuel Huntington believed that civilian control of the military should extend no further than laws and budgets, in other words, checks and balances that maintain civilian control over the military. This theory assumes a professional force isolated from the civilian population, whose policies and day-to-day operations are governed by the chain of command (Huntington 1985). Huntington's theory is called the Liberal Theory, because he believed that infusion liberal ideas and theories (imposing social agendas on the military) could ultimately damage the ability America's armed forces to accomplish their primary mission of securing the country (Feaver 1996).

Huntington's theory of civil-military relations is exemplified in the integration of the Army during the Korean War. Although there was an effort in the civilian sector calling for the full integration of African Americans into Army units, the action did not actually take place until General Ridgeway decided that such an action was in the best interest of the Army to do so, do to manpower shortages (Nalty and Macgregor 1985).

25

Here, a military professional determined what was good for the military and acted according to the military's primary mission.

Morris Janowitz, in his Republican Theory, posited that effective civilian control of the military comes from the complete integration of the military into civil life (Janowitz 1960). This would mean that there would be no military housing on bases, but the troops would live out among the population. There would be no garrison communities (Snider and Carlton-Carew 1995). The idea of a professional soldier would give way to that of the citizen-soldier, which in turn would result in the military being more representative of civilian opinion and norms. According to the theory, this would better ensure the military resembled the civilian populace that by law controls it.

An example of the Janowitz theory in practice is the repeal of the ―Don't Ask, Don't Tell Act." In this case the civilian authority mandated that the military change its policies in order to ensure the military operates more in accordance to the civilian sector and with what the majority of what the civilian population believes is fair.

These two theories are essential to this study because they address a question that underlies this whole body of research: Now that laws have been enacted to ensure that persons of any ethnicity may join the Army, in any capacity in which an individual qualifies; if the Army is currently fighting and winning the nation's wars effectively; is it obligated to allocate resources to ensuring that all of its branches reflect the civilian ethnic demographic?

Chapter Summary

African American service in American history and the circumstances that surrounded it shaped the cultural attitude that many African Americans bear toward the military. Since the military is perceived as a socioeconomic stepping stone to other rewarding careers, the utility of service in the maneuver branches is lost on many African American cadets. Previous studies on the subject of low African American representation in the maneuver branches detail the problem and cite the lack of proper mentorship as one of the problems. Deliberate mentorship, applied to address the basic assumptions about service in Armor and Infantry, can decrease the problem over time. Lastly, civil-military theorist Huntington and Janowitz supply two different methods of civil control of the military that differ on what role the Army must play in advancing social issues. MCoE and Army leaders must determine under which theory the Army will address minority representation in the maneuver branches.

CHAPTER 3

RESEARCH METHODOLOGY

This chapter describes the methods used to develop and analyze a theoretical

program that can influence African American cadets to choose Armor or Infantry as their

branch. The steps are: validate the problem exists, determine probable causes, select and

define one critical or key cause, propose a detailed solution to the problem, and analyze

the acceptability, suitability and feasibility of the proposed solution.

Validating the Problem

The impetus for this study was a comment made by the Chief of Armor, Brigadier

General Ted Martin when he addressed the Armor officers assigned to the summer

Intermediate Level Education class of 2011. Brigadier General Martin stated that he did

not like the fact that Armor branch was only assessing ten African American second

lieutenants into the branch cohort 2010 (Martin 2010). He considered this a problem,

given the large pool of African American cadets assessed into the officer ranks. Two

questions resulted from this one instance: is this occurrence unique to this branch at a

point in time or is this a phenomenon that occurs on a perennial basis, and if this is a

consistent occurrence, does the Army as an institution consider it a problem and why.

The answers to these two questions were found in open source literature, and

Cadet Command data detailing low African American participation in combat arms. The

data showed that this was a continuous problem and the fact that Cadet Command had

conducted a study on it proved that the Army considered it a challenge (Huggins 2010).

Popular literature such as magazine and newspaper articles that addressed the low number of African American officers also indicated that the topic had the propensity to create negative perceptions of the Army in the civilian sector. An Army officer diversity briefing on the importance of officer diversity throughout the Army specified why the Army believes that diversity is important (Sayles 2010).

These documents validated the problem as not particular to the Armor Branch, but across all the maneuver branches. In order to limit the scope of the study and produce a recommendation actionable by a specific body, the study focuses on low African American cadet interest in Infantry and Armor. Doing so allowed the analysis to produce information upon which recommendations, actionable by the MCoE leadership, can be made.

Determining Probable Causes of the Problem and
Selecting a Course of Action Theme

Data on the probable causes of the problem consisted of two themes: culture, and mentorship (Butler 1996; Harney 2000; Burke 2002; Smith 2006; Huggins 2010). Discussion of culture primarily dealt with the culture of the African American community and its attitude toward service in the Army. Within this culture it appears that a majority of African American cadets join the Army in order to gain skills for future careers in the civilian sector. Further, African American cadets did not perceive the maneuver branches as providing those skills (Lim et al. 2009).

The second cultural cause of the problem specifically concerns assessing cadets from Historically Black Colleges and Universities in maneuver branches. The differences between Historically Black College and University culture and Army culture were not being addressed during cadet training, therefore, African American cadets lagged behind their white counterparts in training scores and thus their place on ROTC Order of Merit lists (Butler 1996; Burke 2002). Key to these findings was that in nearly all of the studies conducted by military officers, improved mentorship was found to be critical in addressing the cultural issues.

The lack of mentorship of the Army's junior leaders is cited as a cause of both low accession and retention of minority officers in the maneuver branches (Butler 1996; Harney 2000). Mentoring programs provide role models for young cadets and officers to emulate and should increase the propensity for African Americans to join the maneuver branches (Clark 2000). Such programs also teach all cadets about Army norms that may differ from their ethnic or community norms, which allows the cadets to better operate in the Army environment. Since this was a recurring theme within the available literature, it led to developing a mentorship based solution to changing African American perceptions about the maneuver branches.

Proposing a Solution to the Problem

In proposing a mentorship solution to a cultural problem, the study had to define what culture is and how mentorship is effectively conducted. Since the Army teaches organizational culture at CGSC, the study utilizes that model in order to make it more familiar to leaders within the MCoE. The cultural model consists of three levels that encompass an organization's values and beliefs, basic underlying assumptions, and ultimately artifacts, which are the outward symbols of the organization (Schein 1992). Using data that depicts the African American community's culture as it pertains to the Army, the study populated Schein's cultural model with the values, underlying assumptions and artifacts of African American community, in order to provide a graphic

30

representation of the problem that the maneuver branches are facing (Lim et al. 2009). In short, the model presented the African American Community's perception of the utility of serving in the maneuver branches as the key cause of a lack of African American interest in serving in Infantry and Armor. This became the point of attack for the proposed mentorship program. Next, the study had to determine what defines effective mentorship.

Data on effective mentorship derived from primary sources stated that mentorship had to be consistent and that the mentor and the protégé had to be compatible (Ensher 2005; Johnson and Ridley 2004). Mentorship provided the protégé with a better understanding of his working environment and the ability to make more informed choices about his professional future (Thomas and Thomas 2010). Such mentorship was found to be especially important for minority success in the Army (Dreher and Cox 1996). Lastly, mentorship was found to be a part of the Army's leadership model which made a mentorship solution to the problem an acceptable option (DA 2006).

A proposed solution to the problem was then developed by determining how the tenets of effective mentorship could be applied to changing the negative African American perception of the utility of serving in the maneuver branches. Using the data from the Cadet Command study that finds that the majority of cadets make their branching decision early in their cadet careers, and that those cadets that do choose to be a part of a mentorship program primarily choose active duty cadre to be their mentors. Therefore, this study proposed that the MCoE assign a larger number of successful post command captains and majors to pre-commissioning sources as Assistant Professors of

Military Science (APMS) to provide the mentorship necessary to properly inform branch choice. Next this solution had to be evaluated by Army standards.

Evaluating the Proposed Solution

The basis of analysis for the mentorship program was taken from Army doctrine because the intended audience for this study is Army leadership. Field Manual 5.0 dictates three criteria for analysis of a solution or COA: suitability, acceptability, and feasibility (DA 2006). The Army's definition of suitability is —can accomplish the commander's intent and planning guidance" (DA 2010, B-14). In regard to this study, suitability refers to the proposed formal mentoring program possibly persuading more African American cadets to branch Armor or Infantry. Suitability of the COA was analyzed first because it determines whether the mentorship solution even addresses the cultural problem facing the Army.

Acceptability is determined by assessing whether the COA is —proportional and worth the cost in personnel, equipment, materiel, time involved, or position . . . and is militarily and politically supportable" (DoD 2010, 1). This joint definition is used because the definition in Field Manual 5.0 applies to an operational COA and therefore is too broad to address the implementation of a mentorship COA. The risks associated with this COA were found to be political and associated with the Army's leadership development model.

Feasibility is defined as accomplishing the mission within the established time, space, and resource limitations (DA 2010, B-14). For the purposes of this study, feasibility of the proposed mentorship program is analyzed by addressing maneuver force manning and the priorities of the Army which determines the assignment of officers to various positions.

The COA was initially found to be suitable because it specifically addressed the key cause of low African American interest in Infantry and Armor, but this finding was disputed by Cadet Command findings that mentorship had little effect on cadets' branch choices (Huggins 2010). This conflict in findings led to a deeper investigation into mentorship in ROTC. Findings that cadet interest in mentorship has dropped sharply since the Army increased use of contractors as APMSes, then prompted further investigation into ROTC's use of contractors (Huggins 2010; Smith III 2010). Findings that the use of contractors to teach the youngest of the Army's officers may be detrimental to the future of the Army's Officer Corps, suggested that it may be the contractors that bias the Cadet Command findings (Colarusso, Lyle, and Wardinski 2010). Therefore, the findings of Cadet Command did not change this study's evaluation that the Mentorship COA was suitable. Next the COA's acceptability was evaluated.

The Mentorship COA was found to be acceptable in the study's analysis, because, as defined, there were no political or public affairs risks present should the program be implemented. Also, implementation of such a program only requires manpower available after the Army fills its operational billet, which does not unduly put the Army's primary mission at risk. A risk that cannot be analyzed by this study is the effect of allowing their most high potential officers to fill broadening assignments outside of the operational realm. That is the primary question of the program's acceptability and one that can only be answered by the MCoE leadership. The feasibility of implementing such a program was analyzed next.

Feasibility was determined by studying the ability of the maneuver branches to staff such a program across a wide number of pre-commissioning sources in the current Army operating environment. Analysis of unit manning priorities, data taken from the Army's organizational database, and branch demographics proved that the branches were challenged to fill the current operational billets due to the large amount of maneuver officers required to conduct combat operations (Farrisee 2008, USAFMSA 2011; Armor 2010; Eliassen 2010). Despite the challenges, Armor and Infantry filled the top priority billets and still had officers to assign to other lower priority billets including ROTC and USMA. But both branches had a low number of captains and majors assigned to ROTC relative to the branch numbers (Evans 2011; Eliassen 2010). Thus a study of the maneuver branch assignment methodology was necessary.

The data provided by Armor Branch's January 2010 Branch Brief did not adequately explain why more officers were not assigned to ROTC billets (Armor 2011). Thus the study had to analyze the culture of the maneuver branches in order to understand what their values were as it pertained to officer management. The most expedient way to analyze the culture of the branches was to study the way they select officers for battalion command. Using statistics from an Armor Branch Command Selection Board analysis memorandum, the study found that more officers are not assigned to ROTC billets because the branch cultures do not value that position as one that prepares and officer for battalion command. This was enough to assess the COA as infeasible.

Since the Mentorship COA was found to be infeasible in the Army's current operating environment due to manning priorities and the culture of maneuver, the study had to conclude with recommendations of how make this COA feasible and how to proceed with other COAs within the current operational environment.

In order to make these recommendations, this study framed the problem in the context of two widely know theories of civil-military relations. Samuel Huntington's Liberal Theory and Morris Janowitz's Republican Theory (Huntington 1985; Janowitz 1960). By couching the Army's options within the framework of these two theorists, this study concluded with decisions that the MCoE and the Army may eventually have to make.

Chapter Summary

This research methodology can be duplicated, but because the study analyzes attitudes of cultures, regulations and norms that can change over time, the same methodology conducted at a later date does not guarantee the same findings. Cultures change and Army regulations change, but applying the methodology of validating the problem, determining the causes, proposing and analyzing a solution should lead future researchers to defendable conclusions to this question.

CHAPTER 4

ANALYSIS

Introduction

In attracting more African Americans to the maneuver branches, Infantry and Armor branches should establish a formal mentorship program implemented by successful post-command captains and majors assigned to assistant professor of military science billets at ROTC or similar positions at the USMA. The first section of this chapter proposes such a mentorship program and the messages that it should contain.

This research then addresses the suitability, acceptability and feasibility of implementing the described program in the current Army operating environment. This includes dissecting the Army officer assignments process, the Army manning priority and the culture of Army assignments within the maneuver branches.

Developing a Proposed Mentorship Program

The mentorship program that this study proposes is tailored to address the cultural causes of low African American interest in joining the maneuver branches. These causes can be couched in Schein's model of organizational culture which is outlined in chapter 2. Figure 3 depicts the African American culture as it pertains to service in the Army using Schein's model. When portrayed as such the key cause of low African American interest in the maneuver branches becomes evident.

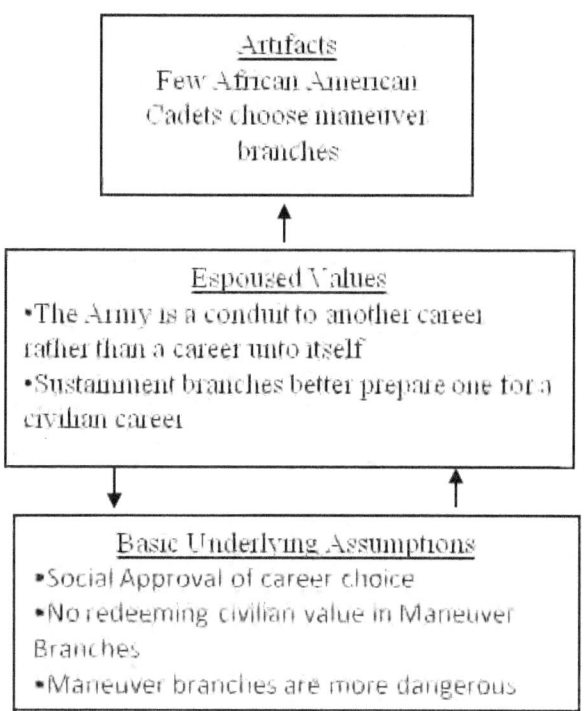

Figure 3.   African American Culture Model as it Pertains to Branch Choice
Source: Created by author. The African American Culture as it pertains to branch choice is based on the belief that maneuver branches do not prepare one properly for a successful civilian career.

The mentorship program directly addresses the basic underlying assumptions that there is no redeeming value in joining Armor or Infantry and that the maneuver branches are more dangerous than other branches. Secondarily, the program would also mentor cadets more deeply in the Army culture. This secondary mentorship goal would pertain more to cadets who are in ROTC at Historically Black Colleges and Universities and who are not conducting daily business in a white majority setting.

The Personnel

Recommended personnel to fill assistant Professor of Military Science billets in order to implement the mentorship program would be successful post-company command captains, majors awaiting assignment to Intermediate Level Education, or majors who have completed successful Key Developmental jobs. At the outset of this program, it is preferred that the officers be African Americans. As the program continues, eligible officers of all races should be given equal consideration.

Maneuver branch managers or the branch chiefs should screen Officer Evaluation Reports to ensure that only quality officers are assigned to potential mentoring posts. If the Army chooses its Professors of Military Science through a board process, then the Maneuver branches should ensure that they are sending their strongest officers to assist in mentoring the finest cadets to consider joining Armor or Infantry. Additionally, the rigor of mentoring and the mental deftness it requires to persuade and train young cadets demands strong officers.

The preference of African American mentors to initially fill these assignments is based on research that —Rotégés of color specifically acknowledge the importance of having mentors of their own ethnicity" (Ensher and Murphy 2005, 206). This is because African American to African American mentorship may provide additional comfort to both parties due to commonality in identification and experiences (Johnson and Ridley 2004). The MCoE should consider that African American mentors may be more effective at Historically Black Colleges and Universities, because those mentors would initially be more comfortable operating in an environment that is majority African American. Also, these African American officers should have a better grasp of both the African American culture they are operating in and the Army culture which they are teaching.

An inability to identify enough African American officers to assign to such billets should not deter either of the maneuver branches from implementing a mentorship

38

program. General Colin Powell and other senior military leaders, in recounting their own experiences, have stressed that African American mentors are not absolutely necessary since good mentorship can be provided by officers of any ethnicity (Baldor 2008). Despite the ethnicity of the mentor or the cadet, the need for mentorship directed toward the appropriate choice of branch is the main priority.

The Messages

Army officers who have served between 2002 and 2011 have done so in an operational environment reliant on themes and messages. These messages, delivered on a consistent basis, are meant to convince the target audience of the Army's values and steer them toward the institution's desired end state. Deliberate mentorship should contain similar messages that instill the values and beliefs of the institution, so that the mentee has an increased chance of success. In the case of this study, the messages that maneuver mentors use should espouse the wider Army values, advise about the Army culture and how it is similar or different from the culture that the protégé is used to operating in, and tout the utility of service in Infantry or Armor in pursuit of an Army or civilian career.

Of the three messages above, the conveyance of the latter two are the most important for the mentor to ensure. This is not to diminish the importance of the Army values, but those values are addressed in leadership classes in the ROTC and USMA curriculums (Harney 2000). Coping and succeeding in an Army culture that may differ from the one an African American cadet is used to is not in either curriculum, but is described as a source of consternation for African American cadets not used to accustomed to a majority white setting (Butler 1996). This is where a maneuver mentor

39

may be able to assist the cadet in better assimilating to the Army; especially a mentor who is aware of both the Army and the African American culture way.

Maneuver mentors would also be instrumental in touting the advantages inherent in branching Infantry or Armor. For those who intend to make the Army a career, these mentors must mention that the majority of the three and four-star positions within the force are held by former maneuver officers (GOMO 2010a). For those using service in the Army as a stepping stone to a more lucrative career, the mentor should inform the cadet of the wide range of duties that maneuver leaders encounter during their service.

Infantry and Armor junior officers serving in Modified Table of Organization and Equipment or _line' units are afforded the opportunity to gain knowledge and limited expertise in almost every aspect of how the Army operates. The mentor could compare the duties of a maneuver junior officer to that of a Medical Service Corps officer of the same grade. This branch is the most popular among non-white cadets (Huggins 2010).

Where the mentors would need support from the Department of the Army, is in identifying former maneuver officers who are prospering in the civilian sector. If the mentors are able to include actual examples of successful civilians who used to be maneuverists into their messages, it may better influence cadets. Currently, Armor branch has identified several African American maneuver officers who have been successful within the Army, but what is lacking is the pictures and biographies of African Americans succeeding in the civilian sector, who were former maneuver officers (Evans 2011).

Suitability: Does the Proposed Solution Fit the Problem?

Addressing Root Causes of African American
Attitudes toward Maneuver

The primary cause of African American reluctance to join the maneuver branches is the perceived lack of utility for pursuing future civilian careers (Huggins 2010). The third message used in the proposed mentorship program directly addresses that perception. If that message is given persistently from the beginning of a cadet's college tenure, there is a possibility that that cadet could be influenced to join the maneuver branches. This assessment is based on the Army Cadet Command's most recent study that finds most cadets choose a branch a service by the first or second year of their ROTC experience (Huggins 2010, 85).

The message concerning how to succeed in the Army culture also fits within the intent of the mentorship program, because it should increase cadets' success at Basic and Advance Camp during the pre-commissioning process. This message is especially applicable to situations where cadets are not in a majority white environment during the school year (Burke 2002).

The mentorship program would provide suitable maneuver role models for cadets. If Infantry and Armor are able to muster enough successful African American officers to serve as APMSes, tactical officers or instructors at USMA, then it would provide the African American maneuver role models that other studies cite as useful for recruitment of cadets into those branches (Butler 1996; Burke 2002; Harney 2000).

Adherence to the Army Mentorship Construct

One way that Field Manual 6-22 the Army's leadership manual Field Manual

defines mentorship is —sharig the benefit of their perspective and experience" (DA 2006,

12-11). Such sharing of experiences from senior to junior professionals should include

recommendations on what to study, on what to focus, and to whom the protégé may look

to as an example to emulate (DA 2006, 12-12). The very implementation of a mentorship

program with the appropriate messages adheres to the Army's leadership construct.

Findings That Diminish the Role of Mentorship
in Branch Choice

Cadet Command's 2010 study on cadet branch choices found mentorship's role in

the process to be minimal among all ethnicities, except in the case of cadets who opted to

serve in the Infantry (Huggins 2010, 19). Trends in regards to Infantry do not translate

when applied solely to African American Cadets. Of 43 African American cadets

surveyed who had Infantry mentors, only five chose Infantry as their branch of choice. Of

the nine cadets who identified their mentors as Armor officers, two eventually branched

Armor (Huggins 2010, 7). Such findings cast doubt on the suitability of applying

mentorship to the phenomenon of low African American interest in branching maneuver.

But elements impacting cadets' desire for mentorship and perhaps the quality of

mentorship offered must be addressed.

Beginning in 2000, the Army began to hire an increasing amount of contractors to

fill ROTC positions left vacant due to personnel cuts in the 1990s, and the increase of

operational deployments (Wardinski, Lyle, and Colarusso 2010, 11). This change in

manning may have had the unintended effects of decreasing cadets' desire for mentorship (because of the lack of a uniformed active duty officer), and increasing the number of cadets that the Professor of Military Science, or the Training Noncommissioned Officer must mentor. The same report that states that mentorship does not appear to be a factor in branching decisions also states that the number of third-year cadets who have elected to have a mentor has declined over 40 percent since 2000 (Huggins 2010, 16). The Army's stopgap measure to maintain the size of ROTC faculty has not proven to maintain the same level of cadet confidence in the cadre.

Cadets may not have enough institutional knowledge or experience to recognize that a contractor, who is former military, may have the same amount of knowledge as a uniformed cadre, and thus not choose to trust in that contractor for career advice. Dr. Huggins' 2010 report states those cadets who do choose to be mentored, generally choose their active duty PMSes or the Non-commissioned officers as mentors (Huggins 2010, 16). Additionally, contractors may not invest the same energy in mentoring cadets for service as officers as an active duty officer in the same position would. COL Irving Smith III, a professor at USMA, also suggests that there may be a difference in the quality of leadership that ROTC cadets are receiving due to the use of contractors.

> ROTC cadets now receive much of their exposure to and understanding of the Army from these contract personnel, while West Point cadets continue to receive their exposure to and understanding of the Army from a hand-picked cadre of active duty officers all of whom have at least a master's degree. Without denigrating the quality of contractor ROTC cadre, it appears that, in the aggregate, black officers commissioned through ROTC are probably not being exposed to the same quality of faculty as those commissioned through West Point. (Smith 2010, 40)

These factors must be considered when assessing the utility of mentorship in branching.

In summary, the proposed construct of the mentorship program is suitable to the intent of increasing African American cadet knowledge about the advantages of branching maneuver, while simultaneously assisting them in adjusting to Army culture and norms. What is questionable is the suitability of mentorship as a solution to the problem of low African American interest in Infantry or Armor as evidenced by Cadet Command's recent study. But factors such as when, how and whom is conducting the mentorship should be studied further before passing final judgment on mentorship as a suitable COA.

Acceptability: Is it Worth the Cost and Associated Risks?

The monetary cost of such a program is worth the advantage of attracting the pre-commissioning sources' best and brightest cadets to the maneuver branches, because the cost of assigning officers as APMSes is comparable to the cost of assigning them anywhere else in the Army. To explain, the Army is going to reassign an officer after successful company command or three years at a duty station as a matter of policy. So, it will incur a cost of moving the officer whether this officer is assigned to a pre-commissioning node or not. Therefore, this study does not have in depth evaluation of the monetary cost associated with implementing the Mentorship COA.

Defining the Risks

There are two risk categories in assigning high-potential captains and majors to the pre-commissioning sources: Political risk and leadership development risks. The political risk of implementing a Mentorship COA involves how the program is advertised to the wider community. Due to a low approval rating of affirmative action-like hiring practices, this program could be construed as a type of targeted hiring practice, exclusive of non-minority cadets and causing public discontent with the Army (UPI 2010). While it is true that the cause for the COA's implementation would be the lack of African American cadets who choose maneuver as their branches of service, the program, as defined, benefits all cadets. Every cadet in the pre-commissioning nodes will have the same access to knowledgeable captains and majors. In essence, rather than being a program directed solely at minorities, such a program would be greatly beneficial to the entire pre-commissioning cohort. Ensuring that wider Army leadership and the public knows this fact is critical to mitigating the political risk of this COA.

The leadership development risk cannot be immediately evaluated, as it is something that would have to be studied over time after implementation. The risk is that removing high-potential captains and majors from the operational force for a period of two to three years may leave them less prepared for successful battalion command or service on higher level staffs. This is a risk that the MCoE leadership must weigh against the possible outcome of attracting the best and brightest cadets from all ethnicities into its ranks. Although this risk cannot be evaluated by this study, assignment of officers to non-traditional operations billets is not an idea foreign to the Army. In fact MCoE could lead the way for the Army's transformation of the Officer Personnel Management System (Tice 2010).

As of January, 2010, HRC and Army leaders were assessing ways to overhaul the officer professional development system, including giving officers a more diverse array of —assignment experiences" (Tice 2010, 1). These experiences would give officers more time for personal, professional, and educational growth without endangering their chances for promotion and battalion command (Tice 2010, 1). By using successful officers in APMS billets, Armor and Infantry could lead the way in changing the officer management model for the Army. Current cultural barriers to this type of action are examined in the feasibility portion of this chapter.

Summarily, the Mentorship COA is low risk politically if the program is correctly advertised and implementation of such a program would force the MCoE to be the vanguard of a new officer professional development model that may soon be implemented. Therefore it is an acceptable course of action.

Feasibility: Can the Maneuver Branches Implement the Program?

Manning

Number of Pre-Commissioning Nodes vs. Available Pool of Officers

The Army's largest pre-commissioning program, ROTC, has 273 programs nationwide utilizing approximately 501 captains and majors in Assistant Professor of Military Science billets (Cadet Command 2011; USAFMSA 2011). USMA is authorized 280 captains and majors to fill instructor and tactical officer positions. Of these 280, 175 are coded branch immaterial or combat arms immaterial (USAFMSA 2011). In summary there are almost 700 billets authorized by the army in which the officer may frequently interact with some 24,000 cadets (Cadet Command 2011). Currently, the maneuver branches are not able to take advantage of this large amount of potential mentoring positions, because of competing Army manning priorities, and branch cultures that dictate their assignment methodology.

Priorities

The Army Chief of Staff periodically issues Department of the Army's Manning Guidance, which lays out the Army's priorities for filling unit personnel requirements

(HRC 2011). This guidance provides Army Human Resources branch managers with a template that determines which units will be filled to capacity or over capacity first (see figure 4).

Deployers			
(manning Goal ≥ 100% Assigned)			
GRF/PTDO BCTs	USCENTCOM	ARCENT HQ 93%	
Transition Teams	MNF-I	Special Mission Units	
Deploying Units	MNC-I	USASOC	
See Specified Policy	MNSTC-I	USSOCOM	
	CSTCA		
Priority Missions			
(manning Goal ≥ 90%-100% Assigned)			
USAFRICOM HQ⁺	IET CDR/XO⁺	Old Guard	CCMRF BCT⁺
PMS	WTU Cadre⁺	AETF (5/1 AD)	20th Support Command
Recruiters⁺	TT Training BDE⁺ USA Element	JTF-GTMO	(Chemical, Biological,
USAREC Co CDRs⁺	WHCA	RTB	Radiological, Nuclear,
Drill Sergeants⁺	NATO PE	EUSA (-OCPK)	or High Explosive
	JIEDDO	ARNORTH	[CBRNE])
Remainder of Units			
(filled in accordance with available Army inventory)			

Figure 4.   Manning Priority Guidance and Standards
Source: Gina S. Farrisee, HQDA Active Component Manning Guidance FY 2008-2010 (Washington, DC: Department of the Army, 2008), 4.The chart depicts the units and commands that have priority of manning in FY 2008 through 2010. These units require a large number of maneuver personnel.

Units deploying in support of the country's ongoing conflicts rightfully are first in priority of fill, followed by other missions deemed important by the Department of the Army. These are the billets that the Infantry and Armor branch managers must fill with available officers first, and the demand for maneuver officers is very high under the modular Brigade Combat Team (BCT) system. As of Fiscal Year 2010, there are 45 active component BCTs (DOD Website 2009). In the current Army Force Generation

System, this equates to approximately 12 BCTs currently deployed, 12 BCTs are preparing for deployment, and 12 BCTs have just returned from deployment. The additional nine BCTs are under development as part of the Army's modularization program. Under this schema, 24 BCTs' officer authorizations must be filled at a level no less than 80 percent (Farrisse 2008).

This is the reason that assigning post-command captains and junior majors to pre-commissioning sources becomes a challenge for the maneuver branches. Considering an 80 percent fill of 24 BCTs alone, Armor and Infantry must allocate approximately 563 captains and 172 majors to these priority billets (USAFMSA 2011). In practice, many of the deployed or deploying BCTs are filled to at least 100 percent authorization. These figures do not account for the numerous combat arms captain and major positions that the maneuver branches then have to fill at the Combatant Command, theater and Corps level staffs, which are also listed as priorities in the manning guidance. For a branch such as Armor, which has approximately 700 post-command captains and majors in the force, the named manning priorities severely tax the available pool of officers (Armor 2010). When the requirement to send eligible officers of these grades to CGSC for a year is added, and officers unable to fill deployable billets due to injury or personal challenges, are taken into account, then it becomes easier to understand why a branch such as Infantry can only allocate a total of 17 majors and captains to serve as APMSes in ROTC (Eliason 2010). Armor branch has been able to do a little better with 25 APMSes and 25 Professors of Military Science total in ROTC (Evans 2011).

Understandably, the Army's current responsibility to defend the nation consumes the majority of its maneuver branches' manpower resources. Therefore, when analyzing the feasibility of manning pre-commissioning billets to a level where effective and persistent mentoring can occur, one may consider the mentorship COA infeasible. But there are other factors that the Army has more control over that also contribute to the manning issue. These are the Assignment Methodology, which directly correlates to the larger issue, which is the culture of the maneuver branches.

Culture of Maneuver Branches

The primary mission of both Infantry and Armor is to close with and destroy the enemy through fire and maneuver. They are branches of decisive action where artful command and mastery of doctrine are essential. Therefore, assignments that allow the maneuver officer to hone his command skills and increase his mastery of Army doctrine are considered key to his professional development and essential if he is aspires to assume Battalion Command. Attainment of Battalion Command is considered success within these two branches for those who choose to remain in the Army after company command. The artifact used to define the maneuver culture's values and beliefs is the Fiscal Year 2010 analysis of the Lieutenant Colonel Command Selection List for Armor Officers (Director, Office of the Chief of Armor 2009).

The Lieutenant Colonel Command Selection List Analysis for Armor officers details the selection patterns for command on the last board. These patterns are then used by the Human Resources Command branch managers to assist current captains and majors in attaining future success (Battalion Command). In terms of culture, these analyses bring out the values of the maneuver branches, which preclude branch managers from assigning high potential captains and majors to ROTC positions. Table 1 is a graphical representation of the analysis's findings.

The maneuver branches favor keeping high potential officers within the operational realm of the Army (table 1). In Army colloquialism, the term operational refers to units or jobs that are directly involved with the day to day warfighting functions of the force. This excludes assignments such as an Observer/Controller, or Small Group Instructor. But this study includes both of these jobs in the term operational because Armor and Infantry view them as good positions to maintain and refine one's doctrinal knowledge. That is why potentially successful officers are mentored to seek these positions as their broadening assignments, and it explains why 22 of the 39 FY 2010 selectees had one of these two jobs. APMS is not listed as one of the jobs that any of the selectees held. Thus it appears that position is not valued or considered a key broadening assignment within the maneuver realm.

Table 1: Previous Positions of FY10 Battalion Command Select Armor Officers		
39 Total Armor Officers Selected for Bn CMD in FY10		
Position	# Selectees	Avg Timeframe
CGSC	39	1 Year
SAMS	8	1 Year
Operational Unit Company Command (19-40 MOS)	38	2-4 Years
Training Unit Company Command	1	2 years
Major Key Development in Operational Unit	38	2 Years
Major Key Development in Training Unit	1	2 Years
Small Group Instructor	11	2-3 Years
USMA	5	5 Years
Observer/Controller	11	2-3 Years
24-30 MOS Key Development	24	2-2.5 Years
30+ MOS Key Development	15	3 years
Military Transition Team	5	1 year
M.A.	38	1-2 Years
JOINT	5	2 Years
Aide	8	1-2 Years

Source: Created by author. This table depicts the patterns of jobs held by FY 2010 Armor Battalion Command Selectees.

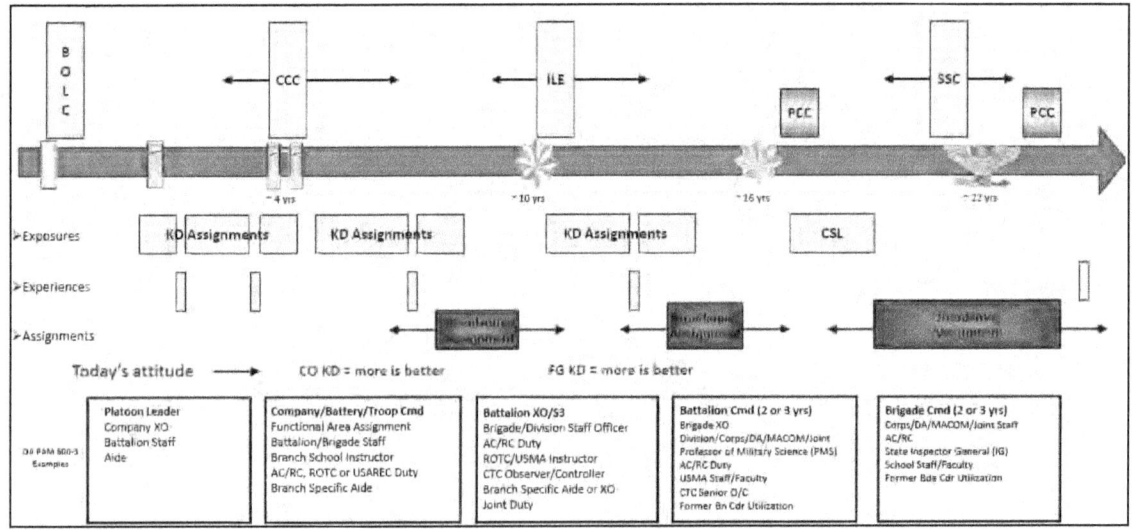

Figure 5.   Officer Career Timeline
Source: Armor Branch, ‑Armor Branch Brief" (Fort Benning, January 2010), 13. The timeline depicts a general professional path of a maneuver officer over time, depicting the positions that an officer is likely to fill at each rank.

Figure 5 shows the typical maneuver officer timeline as depicted in Armor branches January, 2010 branch brief (Armor 2010). Between the end of 24 months of company command and promotion to Lieutenant Colonel, an officer has approximately eight years to amass suitable positions to be considered for battalion command. Of those, one year for CGSC and two years to serve in key developmental positions can automatically be deducted. This leaves five years for broadening assignments. One to two of those years will most likely be served on an operational staff. Assuming that a broadening assignment lasts three years, this leaves the officer and the branch manager one assignment to serve the needs of the Army, foster professional growth and prepare that officer to be competitive on a battalion command selection board. By analyzing the board results analysis, it is clear that neither the officer nor the branch manager would be comfortable in filling an ROTC assignment with the officers who would be competitive for future battalion command.

Maneuver branch culture clearly advocates that its most successful officers should remain within the operational realm throughout their career. APMS positions are not included in that realm. Therefore, assigning successful maneuver officers to ROTC positions would not be supported by senior MCoE leadership.

In summary, assigning more successful maneuver officers to APMS positions to implement a formal mentorship program is not currently feasible. Human resource demands of the current operational environment and the operational-centric assignment culture of the maneuver branches themselves preclude significant changes to the current allocation of officers to ROTC.

Summary

Since low African American cadet interest in the maneuver branches is a matter of values and beliefs, a formal and deliberate mentorship program implemented by maneuver officers should be a suitable. There is data that disputes mentorship's effectiveness with respect to the phenomena, but that data is based on a system where the mentorship model has been skewed by the use of contractors in the ROTC system. If mentorship is conducted by successful maneuver officers as prescribed in this chapter, then it should effectively address the problem and result in an increase in success of attracting African American cadets.

Since the COA does not require additional monetary resources to implement, and is not politically risky it is an acceptable option to addressing the problem. What has not been evaluated is the risk to the maneuver branches and the Army, by assigning high-

53

potential captains and majors to billets outside the established officer professional development timeline (Tice 2010). Despite this, the current cost and risk associated with this COA makes it acceptable.

The mentorship COA is invalidated by the feasibility criterion. Current Army manning priorities and the number of maneuver officers that are required to fill those priorities leaves few post-command captains and majors to fill positions not listed on the Army's manning guidance. Artifacts of maneuver culture then require that those few high-potential officers available be assigned to broadening assignments that make them competitive for selection to battalion command. Currently ROTC assignments are not among those broadening assignments. Thus, this COA is not actionable without a change to the operational environment, or a change in maneuver branch values.

In the future, there is a possibility that the operational environment will change, lessening the amount of mid-grade officers that the Army needs to prosecute combat operations. This would support the feasibility of a deliberate mentorship program, but it would do little to change the values of the Armor and Infantry branches. Maneuver values will only change if the leaders within the Maneuver Center of Excellence and the Department of the Army make decisions and direct action that causes shifts within these values.

CHAPTER 5

CONCLUSIONS AND RECOMMENDATIONS

Introduction

The focus of this study was to determine the suitability, acceptability and feasibility of maneuver branch implementation of a formal mentorship program at the US Army pre-commissioning sources as a way to increase the number of African American cadets who choose Infantry and Armor as their branches of service. After analysis of the problem framed within the current Army operating environment, this study finds that while a mentorship program implemented by successful post-command maneuver captains and majors is a suitable and acceptable COA, it is not feasible in the current operating environment.

Suitability

The primary determinant of an African American cadet's branch choice was found to be the utility of the branch in preparing one for profitable employment after Army service. Currently African American cadets do not perceive Infantry and Armor branches as the best branches in which to gain the skills needed for a successful civilian career. Since cadets learn much of what they know about the Army from ROTC and USMA cadre, a mentoring program that teaches Army values, Army culture, and the utility of the maneuver branches in preparing for a career outside of the military was found to be a sound solution to changing African American perceptions of Infantry and Armor. Since this is a cultural phenomenon, the assignment of successful maneuver officers who know the value of serving in the maneuver branches to positions where they will have the optimal amount of contact with cadets made the Mentorship COA one that, in theory, has a high probability of success over time.

There is a study suggesting that mentorship does not have as much bearing on a cadets branching decision, but that finding may be influenced by the lack of active duty maneuver officers who are currently assigned to APMS billets in ROTC.

Acceptability

The low political risk and monetary cost of implementing the proposed program in contrast to the possible gains, makes it an acceptable option. Since the program is not discriminatory in which cadets receive the mentorship, it should not arouse any public or governmental furor upon implementation. Secondly there is no difference in cost for the Army in implementing this program if compared to assigning maneuver officers to any other duty stations. What cannot be determined by this study is if the risk of retarding the successful leadership development of high-potential officers is worth accessing the highest performing cadets of all ethnicities into the maneuver branches. This topic is tied to the culture of the maneuver branches and is further discussed in the feasibility portion of this chapter.

Feasibility

The mentorship COA is not feasible due to the high demand for maneuver officers in the operational segment of the Army and due to the current operations-centric culture of the maneuver force. The number of Infantry and Armor mid-level officers is stretched very thin because of operations in two theaters. The limited numbers of high potential officers that the two branches have remaining are culturally barred from serving as APMSes in ROTC. Currently, the culture of Infantry and Armor is one that values the attainment of battalion command. The pattern of assignments for those chosen for battalion command does not include service in ROTC. Thus, successful post-command captains and majors are not prime candidates for APMS positions.

Making the Course of Action Feasible: A question of Huntington or Janowitz

Addressing the feasibility gap in the proposed maneuver mentorship model is a process that must begin at the Maneuver Center of Excellence. Maneuver leaders must decide whether their branches are going to follow the Liberal Theory of Civil-Military relations or the Republican one (Huntington 1985; Janowitz 1960). If maneuver chooses to operate under the liberal theory then it should continue to practice the status quo. The maneuver branches and the Army are currently able to fight and win the nations wars with a relative dearth of African American maneuver officers and generals. Therefore, no manpower and resource intensive actions are required to increase African American officer representation within the Infantry and Armor ranks. In this case the MCoE would allow the discard the mentorship COA.

Alternatively, if the MCoE decides to follow a Republican theory approach to manning its officer corps, where the maneuver branches seek to ensure their demography closely resembles that of the civilian population, then it would require deliberate change to its culture and thus, the way it prioritizes the manning of pre-commissioning sources. Changing the maneuver culture would make the mentorship COA viable.

The recommendations that follow address the question of increasing African American officership in Infantry and Armor within both theories.

Operating within Huntington's Liberal Theory:
Conducting an Economy of Force

If the Army and the maneuver branches determine that increasing the number of

African American officers within their ranks is not within their purview, then it can

choose to implement a solution which could be called the Economy of Force COA. This

solution should follow the model put forth in a 2011 Armor branch study of the

phenomena (Evans 2011). This model advocates that the branch create a program

something akin to an Armor Roadshow. In such a program, the branch would allow

officers en route to or departing from the Captain's Career Course to visit their alma

maters and espouse the values of the maneuver branches and —emphasize better

communication skills training at Historically Black Colleges and Universities and ROTC

universities" (Evans 2011, 21). This program would also improve branch contact with

USMA and improve the branches' presentation at ROTC cadet summer training. Lastly

this program would seek to send Armor battalion commanders and general officers on a

circuit to further tout to utility of branching maneuver.

This program allows the branches to deliberately target the schools that offer them

the most reward for their efforts and it does not alter the current officer assignment

methodology. It also allows the branch to show that there is success to be had by African

Americans in maneuver and that success is very transferable to the civilian sector. This

program, however, has limitations.

The program would rely on visits of limited duration. Since the phenomenon is a

cultural one, then these short visits may not convey the messages with enough frequency

or emphasis to change beliefs and values that have developed within the African

American community over time. In other words, a one day visit may do little to increase the amount of maneuver contact cadets receive and thus may not increase interest in joining Armor or Infantry.

When operating within Huntington's model of civil-military relations, and conducting the Maneuver Road Show, the MCoE should work with Cadet Command to increase the Armor and Infantry APMS presence at the schools that produce the highest numbers of African American Second Lieutenants per year, in order to increase the probability of African American cadets choosing to serve in maneuver. According to the Office of the Chief of Armor's report, the top five ROTC schools that should be considered are South Carolina State University, Florida A&M University, Virginia State University, Morgan State University, and Jackson State University (Evans 2011, 24). In addition, the branches should highly advertise the annual application process to serve as an instructor or tactical officer at USMA, which produces the most African American cadets for the Army per year (Lee 2011).

Operating within Janowitz's Republican Theory:
The Mass Course of Action

Should the Army and maneuver branches decide that it is within the Army's responsibility to do as much as possible to ensure that all the branches within the force represent the demography of the country, then it must change the culture of maneuver. To change the culture of maneuver, several things must happen.

First, Infantry and Armor must reconsider their values and beliefs. They must include the APMS positions within the pool of assignments that they believe make an officer competitive for battalion command. To do this, the branch chiefs and their subordinate representatives must tout the importance of indoctrinating the Army's officer candidates properly. Simultaneously, branch managers who are in charge of assigning officers to different billets must make conscious efforts to assign successful post-command captains and majors to APMS positions and increase the amount of officers that fill those billets. The traits that made these officers successful in their operational units should make them excellent mentors for young cadets.

Secondly the Army and the branches must alter the cultural artifacts that result from current Battalion Command Selection Lists. Currently, what maneuver officers observe from the selection lists is that an APMS position is not one that they should consider if they wish to be a battalion commander. After successful officers have gone to APMS positions and performed well, they should be highly considered when they are on the lists of candidates for battalion command.

Lastly, the branches must do what they have already proposed and conduct the Maneuver Road Shows to explicitly state that they are looking for the best officers of all ethnicities to lead the Army's Infantrymen and Cavalrymen. But these roadshows must not be limited to college campuses. Infantry and Armor leaders must engage the influencers of the African American community who include parents, clergy and educators (Huggins 2010). This series of actions can be called the Mass COA, because the engage a large number of available manpower resources to the problem.

Although fighting and winning the nation's wars remains the priority of the maneuver branches in this COA, reallocating available officer resources to ensure cadets of all ethnicities understand the utility of branching armor and infantry becomes a major shaping operation.

Recommendations for Future Study

1. Attitudes of Minority Officers within the Military: Due to time constraints and the restrictive nature of research concerning human subjects, this study did not use results of surveys or formal interviews. The author was privy to a large number of minority conversations about the topic and the overall experience of minorities in the military. Using these conversations would anecdotally support the findings. However a study that conducted scientific surveys and interviews specifically designed to determine minority attitudes about this topic, and the differences between the white and minority experience within the military, would be helpful in allowing all military leaders to see how different segments of its population view military life and culture. Such a study should be conducted.

2. Effects of Contract ROTC Instructors: Since ROTC is the largest supplier of new officers to the Army, a study of cadet perception of contract instructors should be conducted. Such a study would inform Army leaders on the value of contracting out the indoctrination of the Army's newest officers.

GLOSSARY

Good Old Boy Network. A group of men with a strong sense of fellowship with and loyalty to other members of his peer group. In the military this term is used to denote an informal group of personnel across the rank structure who tend to favor or assist other members of said group

Historically Black Colleges and Universities. Colleges and Universities established before 1964 with the intention of serving the African American Community.

Human Resources Command (HRC). HRC provides the full spectrum of human resources services to Soldiers, veterans, retirees and Army families. The command manages Soldier schooling, promotions, awards, records, transfers, appointments, benefits, and retirement.

Intermediate Level Education (ILE). ILE is the Army's course for majors, preparing them for leadership at the battalion-level and above.

Key Developmental Positions. A position fundamental to the development of an Officer in his or her core branch or functional area competencies or deemed critical by the senior Army leadership to provide experience across the Army's strategic mission.

Maneuver Center of Excellence (MCoE). Located at Fort Benning, GA, the mission of the MCoE is to provide trained, adaptive, and ready Soldiers and leaders for an Army at war, while developing future requirements for the individual Soldier and the Maneuver Force. It is the home of the Infantry and Armor schools and where the Office of the Chief of Infantry, and the Office of the Chief of Armor reside.

REFERENCE LIST

Armor Branch. 2010. Armor branch brief. Fort Benning, January 2010. https://www.hrc.army.mil/site/protect/branches/officer/mfe/armor/brief.htm (accessed 16 April 2011).

Baldor, Lolita C. 1998. Black military officers rare after 60 years of military desegregation. Mindfully.org. http://www.mindfully.org/Reform/2008/Black-Officers-Rare23jul08.htm (accessed 11 March 2011).

Berryman, Sue E. 1988. *Who serves?: The persistent myth of the underclass army.* Boulder, CO: Westview Press.

Bosco, Antoinette, and Peter I. Bosco. 2003. *America at war: World War I.* New York: Facts on File, Inc.

Burke, Emmett E. 2002. Black officer under-representation in combat arms branches. Monograph, School of Advanced Military Studies, Command and General Staff College.

Butler, John Sibley, and Charles C. Moskos. 1996. *All that we can be: Black leadership and racial integration the Army way.* New York: Basic Books.

Butler, Remo. 1995. Why black officers fail in the U.S. Army. Strategy Research Project, U.S. Army War College.

Chambers II, John Whiteclay, and Charles C. Moskos. 1993. *The new conscientious objection: From sacred to secular resistance.* New York: Oxford University Press.

Clark, Ronald P. 2000. The lack of diversity in the infantry: Why are there so few black infantry officers in the U.S. Army? Masters Thesis, United States Army Command and General Staff College.

Colarusso, Michael J., David S. Lyle, and Casey Wardinski. 2010. Accessing talent: The foundation of a U.S. Army officer corps strategy. Monograph, Strategic Studies Institute. http://www.strategicstudiesinstitute.army.mil/pubs/display.cfm?pubID=972 (accessed 29 January 2011)

Department of the Army. 2006. Field Manual 6-22, *Army leadership.* Washington, DC: Department of the Army.

———. 2010. Field Manual 5.0, *The operations process.* Washington, DC: Department of the Army.

Department of Defense. 2010. Joint Publication 1-02, *Department of Defense dictionary of military and associated terms*. Washington, DC: Department of Defense. 8 Novemeber. http://www.dtic.mil/doctrine/new_pubs/jp1_02.pdf. (accessed 19 May 2011).

Director, Office of the Chief of Armor. 2009. FY10 LTC command selection list analysis. 18 May. https://www.benning.army.mil/Armor/OCOA/content/Promotions/FY10%20LTC%20Command%20Selection%20List%20Analysis.pdf (accessed 14 April 2011).

Doward, Oscar W., Jr. 2008. Missing in action: African American combat arms officers in the United States Army. Monograph, School of Advanced Military Studies, Command and General Staff College.

Dreher, George F., and Taylor H. Cox Jr. 1996. Race, gender, and opportunity: A study of compensation attainment and the establishment of mentoring relationships. *Journal of Applied Psychology* 81, no. 3 (June): 297-308.

Dubois, W. E. B. 1918, ―Close Ranks‖. *The Crisis* (July). In *Blacks in the military: Essential documents*. Morris J. MacGregor, and Bernard C. Nalty, 77. Wilmington: Scholarly Resources Inc., 1981.

―――. 1940. *Dusk of dawn: An essay toward an autobiography of a race concept.* New York: Harcourt, Brace and Company.

Eliassen, Michael T. 2011. Phone conversation with author. 4 January.

Ellis, Mark. 2001. *Race war and surveillance: African Americans and the United States government during World War I.* Bloomington, IN: Indiana University Press.

Ensher, Ellen A., and Susan Elaine Murphy. 2005. *Power mentoring: How successful mentors and protégés get the most out of their relationships.* San Francisco: Jossey-Bass.

Evans, J.D. 2011. *Officer diversity and advancement report.* Email with author, 2 March.

Farrisee, Gina S. 2008. *HQDA active component manning guidance FY 2008-2010.* Washington, DC: Department of the Army.

Feaver, Peter D. 1996. The civil military problematique: Huntington, Janowitz, and the question of civilian control. *Armed Forces & Society* 23, no. 2 (winter): 149-178.

Franklin, John Hope, and Alfred A. Moss, Jr. 1994. *From slavery to freedom: A history of African Americans.* 7th ed. New York: McGraw-Hill.

General Officer Management Office. 2010a. *Army general officer public roster (by rank) 1 December, 2010.* Washington, DC: Department of the Army. https://www.gomo.army.mil/ext/portal/default.aspx (accessed 12 December 2010)

————. 2010b. *General officer minority report-total force.* Washington, DC: Department of the Army. https://www.gomo.army.mil/ext/portal/default.aspx (accessed 12 December 2010)

Hall, Kimberly Curry, Nelson Lim, Jefferson P. Marquis, David Schulker, and Xiaohui Zhuo. 2009. *Officer classification and the future of diversity among senior military leaders: A case study of the Army ROTC.* Arlington, VA: RAND.

Harney, Robert A. 2000. Development of a formal Army officer mentorship model for the twenty-first century. Masters Thesis, United States Command and General Staff College.

Huggins, Bert Ph.D. 2010. Branching decisions from cadet surveys. Hampton, VA: Cadet Command.

Johnson, Charles Jr. 2002. *African Americans and ROTC: Military, naval and aeroscience programs at historically black colleges, 1916-1973.* Jefferson: McFarland & Company, Inc., Publishers.

Johnson, W. Brad, and Charles R. Ridley. 2004. *The elements of mentoring.* New York: Palgrave Macmillan.

King, David C., and John Della Volpe. 2008. Attitudes and the formation of attitudes toward the US military. Slide presentation from a lecture at Harvard University. 9 July.

Lee, Rance. 2011. Interview by author, 11 January, Ft. Leavenworth, KS.

Logan, Rayford, Ph.D. 1941. U.S. Congress. Senate. Subcommittee of the Committee on Appropriations, *Military Establishment Appropriations Bill*, 76th Cong., 3rd Sess.. In. *Blacks in the Military: Essential Documents*, edited by Morris J. MacGregor and Bernard C. Nalty, 101.Wilmington: Scholarly Resources Inc., 1981.

MacGregor, Morris J., and Bernard C. Nalty, eds. 1981. *Blacks in the military: Essential documents.* Wilmington: Scholarly Resources Inc.

Martin, Ted. 2010. Chief of armor brief. Lecture, Command and General Staff College, Fort Leavenworth, KS. 3 August 2010.

Maxfield, Betty, D. 2010. *Army demographics: FY09 Army profile.* http://www.armyg1. army.mil/hr/demographics.asp (accessed 10 January 2010).

Myrdal, Gunnar. 1944. *An American dilemma: The negro problem and modern diplomacy.* New York: Harper & Row, Publishers.

Moskos, Charles Jr., ed. 1971. *Public opinion and the military establishment.* Beverly Hills: Sage Publications.

Office of the Secretary of Defense. 1971. *Negro participation in the armed forces and in Southeast Asia.* Washington, DC: Office of the Secretary of Defense. In *Blacks in the military: Essential documents,* edited by Morris J. MacGregor and Bernard C. Nalty, 344-45. Wilmington: Scholarly Resources Inc. 1981.

Pentagon. 1975. *Equal opportunity current news.* August 14. (received in an email message from Mr. Kenneth Madison, 4 October, 2010).

Powell, Colin. 1995. *My American journey.* New York: Random House.

Rostker, Bernard. 2006. *I want you!: The evolution of the all volunteer force.* Santa Monica: RAND Corp.

Schein, Edgar H. 1985. Uncovering the levels of culture. *Organizational Culture and Leadership.* San Francisco: Jossey-Bass, 1992, 16-27. In *L100: Developing organizations and leaders,* 133-144. Fort Leavenworth: US Army Command and General Staff College, 2010.

Smith, Irving III. 2010. Why black officers still fail. *Parameters* 40, no. 3 (Autumn): 32-47.

Shipler, David K. 1997. *A country of strangers: Blacks and Whites in America.* New York: Alfred A. Knopf.

Smith, James M. 2006. Global war on terrorism-the propensity for blacks to serve in the U.S. Army. Monograph, School of Advanced Military Studies, United States Army Command and General Staff College.

Stein, Robert T. 2002. An ant of Reserve Officer Training Corps' program of instruction for future officers. Masters Thesis, United States Army Command and General Staff College.

Terry, Wallace. 1984. *Bloods.* New York: Random House.

Thomas, Ted Ph.D, and Jim Thomas. 2010. *Mentoring coaching and counseling: Toward a common understanding.* Fort Leavenworth: United States Army Command and General Staff College.

Tice, Jim. 2010. Officer's career path to be overhauled. *Army Times.* January 31. https://poky.atpco.com/atp/login.aspx?pubCode=ARM&forward=http%3A%2F%2Fwww.armytimes.com%2Ftnlink.php%3F (accessed 15 April 2011).

Turabian, Kate L. 2007. *A manual for writers.* 7th ed. Chicago: University of Chicago Press.

United Press International. 2010. Poll: voters so-so on affirmative action. http://www.upi.com/Business_News/2010/07/13/Poll-Voters-so-so-on-affirmative-action/UPI-75951279046865/ (accessed 12 May 2011).

United States Army Cadet Command. http://www.rotc.usaac.army.mil (accessed 5 January 2011).

United States Army Command and General Staff College. 2010a. *L100: Developing organizations and leaders.* Fort Leavenworth: US Army Command and General Staff College.

————. 2010b. ST 20-10, *Master of military art and science (MMAS) research and thesis.* Ft. Leavenworth, KS: United States Army Command and General Staff College.

United States Army Force Management Support Agency. 2011. Force management system web site: FMSWeb. https://fmsweb.army.mil/unprotected/splash (accessed 1 April 2011).

United States Army Human Resources Command. 2010. Officer personnel management directorate. https://www.hrc.army.mil/site/Active/opmd.htm (accessed 20 April 2011).

Wallace, Terry. 1984. *Bloods: An oral history of the Vietnam War by black veterans.* New York: Random House.

Williams, Eddie E. 1975. Blacks in the military. *The New York Times*, 2 August. Found in Pentagon. 1975. *Equal Opportunity Current News, 1.* August 14. (received in an email message from Mr. Kenneth Madison on 4 October, 2010).

Wright, Kai. 2002. *Soldiers of freedom: An illustrated history of African Americans in the armed forces.* New York: Black Dog and Leventhal Publishers Inc.

Zachary, Lois J. 2009. *The mentee's guide: Making mentoring work for you.* San Francisco: Jossey-Bass.

www.ingramcontent.com/pod-product-compliance
Lightning Source LLC
Chambersburg PA
CBHW080527290526
45790CB00006B/2324